Dumfries

Through

Glimpses of old

South Machars

Dumfries and Galloway Libraries,
Information and Archives
with Whithorn Photographic Group
1997

First published 1997

Designed by Dumfries and Galloway Libraries, Information and Archives. Set and printed by Solway Offset Services, Catherinefield Industrial Estate, Dumfries for the publisher.

Dumfries and Galloway Libraries, Information and Archives
Central Support Unit, Catherine Street
Dumfries DG1 1JB

Dumfries and Galloway LIBRARIES Information and Archives

ISBN 0 946280 24 X
South Machars is number 3 in the
Dumfries and Galloway : *Through the Lens* series.
For a full list of our publications write to the above address.

ACKNOWLEDGEMENTS

This publication was funded by Groundbase Ltd., the Calouste Gulbenkian Foundation and Dumfries and Galloway Libraries, Information and Archives whose support for this project is greatly appreciated.

Our thanks also to Hilary More of the Department for Community Resources, Dumfries and Galloway Council for her support and help in organising this project.

The following, among others, have generously donated photographs for reproduction; without their help, this volume could not have been published:

John Adair, Jim Allan, Mrs Baxter, Mr D Bell, Ethel Brolls, Dr G Brown, Judy Brown, Rosemary Cameron, Mr and Mrs Chamberlain, Margaret Cronie, Margaret Donaldson, Mrs E Drape, Morag Fisher, Lis Graham, the Herald and Evening Times, Mr and Mrs Jaques, Ruby Kirk, William Lawrie, Mr D Lester, Clifford Longridge, Fiona McLellan, Jock McMaster, Mary McShane, John McWilliam, Mrs M Martin, Mr James Maxwell, Sir Michael Maxwell, Mrs C Millar, John Mills, George Moore, Mrs E J Murray, Miss J Murray, Mr C Sandbach, John Scoular, Mr and Mrs Stewart, Sandra Templeton, Isobel Torbet, Joe Whiteford and the Whithorn Trust.

The plate on page 22 is Crown Copyright: Reproduced by courtesy of Historic Scotland.

PROFITS FROM THE SALE OF THIS BOOK GO TO SUPPORT THE SOUTH MACHARS COMMUNITY CENTRE.

INTRODUCTION

The wealth of photographic material on the Southern Machars has been a constant surprise and pleasure. For each photograph selected, one of equal worth and interest has been left out, in the hope that other volumes can accommodate it in the future.

In this volume, we have ignored a large volume of material on maritime and agricultural subjects, in the attempt to give a general overview of the villages and the great houses of the area between 1890-1945, in a period before economic and social change would alter the balance between the two forever. The two were highly dependent on each other, the villages supplying labour and skilled workmanship, the great houses providing employment and contacts with a wider world.

We are now forced to reconstruct, from the remnants of evidence available to us, a world which was once - and quite recently - taken for granted. Within a few decades, what seemed to be ephemeral pictures of the daily round have become precious historic documents of a vanished way of life and we have become highly aware of the fortunate accidents which have preserved these fragments for the next generation.

We have taken a largely geographical tour of the Southern Machars, following the coast at first and then moving inland, juxtaposing photographs of everyday life with grander pictures of life on the estates.

We hope that this book will contribute to an understanding of that world and argue for the preservation of the evidence relating to it. We hope also that the pleasure we have taken in discovering the changes and comparisons indicated by each picture will be shared and contribute to an enriched understanding of the buildings, countryside and people of the present.

WHITHORN PHOTOGRAPHIC GROUP,
July 1997

MCWILLIAM'S SHOP, ISLE OF WHITHORN

This view, taken in around 1900, shows a characteristic view of the main street, with McWilliam's shop, originally built as a boat-builder's workshop. Outside it stands Andrew McWilliam. The shop, which became a general grocers, as it is today, was well-known for its own blend of tea, as is recorded in the verse:

McWilliam's tea's the best o' a'
It taks the shortest time to dra'
And what is mair
A teaspoon goes as far as twa
O' any ither
What knocked the pimples aff his nose
And gied him courage to propose?
McWilliam's Isle Blend.

ISLE HARBOUR
In 1890, the Isle of Whithorn still carried on an active coastal trade, as these top-sail schooners attest. The buildings on the right were used for storing grain and were still in use in 1938-40, when they served as a canteen for troops at Burrowhead camp. The buildings on the inner quayside were used for unloading coals from Whitehaven.

THE CAIRN, ISLE OF WHITHORN
After World War I, a captured German cannon was placed at the Cairn in lieu of a war memorial. Eventually a war memorial was dedicated in the village, but the cannon survived into the 1940's. Some evacuees, however, found the reminder too distasteful and an attempt was made to push it into the sea. By then, it was in a decayed state and had survived the depredations of generations of Isle children.

TONDERGHIE ROAD, ISLE OF WHITHORN
Here, troops are pictured arriving for Burrowhead, which became a focus of artillery training during World War II. There was also an RAF aerodrome at Kidsdale.

STEAM-THRESHER, BOYACH, ISLE OF WHITHORN

Whithorn Steam Threshing Company was a co-operative, with shares being held by farmers in the South Machars. It was operated by Hugh Smith and Bob Christie and it required as many as nine people, including women and boys, to operate the machine and complete the threshing process. The thresher continued in use until World War II.

THE GOLF HOUSE, ISLE OF WHITHORN

At the turn of the century, there were a great number of local golf courses and tennis courts, many of which are in what we would now consider remote and surprising locations and have now vanished. This picture shows the opening day of play at the Isle of Whithorn course, located at Stein, just north east of the village. Note the magnificent lace bonnets on the two little girls, centre.

KINGCOST WELL, ST. MEDAN'S, MONREITH, 1899

The photographer of this dramatic picture, Gilbert Ritchie, was the fiance of the young lady in the picture, Gordina Nichol. Her father was the skipper of an oyster smack and her mother was a dress-maker. Here she is pictured at the Kingcost well, known for its curative properties of whooping cough, from the old Scots word, *King-cough* or *kink-host*. This folklore is itself an echo of older stories about St. Medana, about whom the miracle is recounted that a healing spring gushed forth when she was obliged to tear out her own eyes, in order to escape the attentions of an admirer.

JOHNNY LOGIE'S CAVE

This wooden shack was built across the mouth of what is now named on the map as the *Hermit's Cave* and was home to Johnny Logie, an ex-miner, who had been partially blinded and suffered deafness as a result of a mining accident. He was a well-educated man and a Stalinist and sought refuge from capitalist society in the remoteness of the Luce Bay coast. Wigtownshire had at one time a number of cave-dwellers, who chose this isolated life for various reasons. Many remember his garden of kelp and the quality of the carrots which grew in the beds; others remember purchasing sea-washed timber from him during World War II, when it was publicly under restriction owing to the war effort. Logie eventually left the cave suffering from pneumonia in 1962. The boy in the picture is William Roddie.

MONREITH VILLAGE
The village grew up surrounding a mill on the Monreith burn. At one point, under the auspices of the Monreith Estate, it had a clay tile and brick works.

SUNDAY SCHOOL PICNIC, LEAVING MONREITH
This Whithorn Sunday School outing in spring carts was obviously a day of festivity, judging by the horses' harness and the holiday clothes. In the background are the wooded policies of the Monreith Estate.

ST MEDAN'S GOLF COURSE

The course was leased from Sir Herbert Maxwell at a peppercorn rent from about the turn of the century. Sir Herbert Maxwell, who is seen here emerging in the lighter suit from the original Club House building, was involved in the design of the course, thanks to his friendship with James Braid, the well-known golf course designer. Eventually, the course was purchased by the Golf Club members from Sir Herbert's grandson, Sir Aymer.

MONREITH HOUSE TENANTRY, 1910
Monreith House, built in 1790 by Alexander Stevens Jnr., is the seat of the Maxwell family. At one time, the Maxwells owned 16,000 acres of farmland in the Machars and a regular feature of agricultural life would have been a gathering of tenants to pay rents on Lady Day in May and at Michaelmas in November and to be entertained to a dinner, garden party or bazaar.

HOUSE PARTY, MONREITH HOUSE, c1890

Sir Herbert Maxwell (1845-1937), who inherited the baronetcy and Monreith estate in 1877, is here shown seated astride the balustrade, outside the extension which he added to the original house, according to a design by Richard Park, Newton Stewart, soon after his inheritance. In line with Sir Herbert's interests in heraldy, the extension has a pediment with armorial bearings and Latin motto; it was largely demolished in 1938. As well as an antiquarian and author, he was also a noted horticulturalist and arboriculturalist and added extensively to the gardens at Monreith.

GARDEN PARTY AT MONREITH, 12th JUNE 1912
This idyllic scene from the eve of the Great War betrays no sign of the changes in land ownership, technology and society which were to come to the countryside after 1918. For the Maxwell family, the War brought tragedy, with the early death on the Front of Captain Aymer, son of Sir Herbert.

GARDEN PARTY AT MONREITH, 12th JUNE 1912
Entertainments and bazaars of this sort continued to be laid on at the House into the 1930's. This photograph shows a rear view of the House and balustraded area, where Sir Herbert had laid out a parterre, with the Latin motto from Job: *Homo quasi Flos egreditur et conteritur.*

AIRLOUR HOUSE
Situated at the edge of the Monreith estate policies, this house was used as a dower house and Herbert Maxwell and his bride, Mary Fletcher Campbell, lived there for some years, while his parents were still alive. The impressive early motor-car dates the picture to the early 1900's.

PORT WILLIAM HARBOUR

Port William village was founded by Sir William Maxwell of Monreith c.1775 and a harbour was built in the 1790's to encourage trade. In this dramatic picture, it would seem that the enlargement of the harbour into a kidney-shape, carried out in 1898 by Henry Walker, factor to the Estate, has been completed. The masted schooners show that coastal trade, including transport of agricultural produce and supplies, was still active, although the smuggling days, during which the village had required a permanent barracks of troops, were long over.

PORT WILLIAM SQUARE

The square has always been the commercial centre of the village, dominated by the Monreith Arms Hotel on the left. Behind the hotel are the traces of the barracks, used to house revenue officers, who battled against a significant smuggling trade along the Luce Bay coast.

GARLIESTON BOAT-BUILDERS

Garlieston was also a model village, founded by the John, Lord Garlies [later the 7th Earl of Galloway] in 1760, as a general improvement to the surroundings of Galloway House. It became a centre for trade with the Cumbrian coast and Liverpool and this photograph shows the traditional craft of the boat-builder around the 1890's In the background, the largest building on the front is the mill, now largely demolished.

EARL OF GALLOWAY WITH TENANTRY 1906

The Earl of Galloway was the largest and most influential landowner on the Machars peninsula. This dinner and rent-day, however, was the last before the Galloway Estates were broken up and sold off, under the burden of extensive debts, and Galloway House occupied by other owners. Note the pipe band in the front row, laid on for the entertainments and the maids in the extreme top right window, watching the proceedings of the photographer.

CASTLEWIGG HOUSE
The seat of the Stewart family, also connected with Tonderghie and Glasserton, Castlewigg House as shown in the picture is a Georgian remodelling of a tower house on the same site. The house was burnt down in 1933 and is now overgrown and ruinous. The gardens were designed by John Claudius Loudon, one of the best-known Victorian writers on plants and gardens. All that is now visible is the ha-ha and some exotic trees; the rest has returned to a state of nature.

CASTLEWIGG HOUSE, INTERIOR OF FRONT HALL
This picture of the interior shows what was lost in the fire. The chair to the right of the door, however, survives in the Old Town Hall at Whithorn and has been used by the burgh and community councils.

SORBIE VILLAGE
This view was taken by J N Alves, the Whithorn photographer, who published many postcards of the area. Sorbie was an L-plan village, also created, like Garlieston, in the late eighteenth century by John, 7th Earl of Galloway. Its Scandinavian name and its tower-house, belonging to the Hannays of Sorbie, however, bear witness to an earlier history.

SMITHY, SORBIE
The smithy at Sorbie was run for 64 years from 1901 to 1965 by Thomas Woods. Here he is shown at the anvil with his brother.

OLD SORBIE CREAMERY
The creameries and their supplying of the milk markets of central Scotland were made possible by their links to the railway network of the Machars. Here old Sorbie creamery is situated adjacent to the tracks and the waiting Glasgow and South-Western goods vans. The station house is behind the fencing, on the left.

BARNBARROCH HOUSE, WHAUPHILL
Once home to the Vans Agnews of Sheuchan and built in 1780, Barnbarroch was burnt to a shell in a disastrous fire of 1942, during which a member of the family died. The ornamental water feature, with the elegant staircase, and extension on the left are presumably the work of John Claudius Loudon, one of the most influential garden designers of his era, who designed gardens and improvements to the house during 1806-8.

WHAUPHILL STATION
A rare view of Whauphill station, which occupied a site to the East of the village main street and is now all but obliterated.

WHAUPHILL INN
The premises run by Mr McCall in the 1890's as an inn are still occupied by the village public house today.

GLASSERTON VILLAGE
The village was built under the architectural influence of nearby Glasserton House and has distinctive diamond panes in the windows of all its houses. The three cottages on the right once included a joiner's workshop and are now amalgamated into one.

BUTLER'S LODGE, GLASSERTON ESTATE
One of the Lodge entrances to Glasserton House, the Lodge has elaborate barge-boards and detailing on the roofing slates. It is now roofless and derelict.

GLASSERTON HOUSE

Demolished c.1940 and leaving virtually no trace, Glasserton, one of the principal residences of the Earls of Galloway, had already been rebuilt on site once in 1740/1 after a fire in 1730, which destroyed its predecessor. This unusual view from the front gardens shows how elegantly the house was set into the surrounding landscape.

21 BIRTHDAY PRESENTATION, GLASSERTON HOUSE

Taken at the rear of Glasserton House, this picture shows a presentation by the estate tenantry to R H Johnston-Stewart (seated centre) on the occasion of his coming of age in 1925. Such presentations were commonplace on the occasions of marriages, engagements and the attaining to majority of the heirs to the large estates.

ELRIG VILLAGE

One of the more remote villages in the Machars, Elrig was nonetheless once the site of a large bone-meal mill and had a wide range of tradesmen and services. After a period of decline, when it seemed destined to abandonment, it is now undergoing a renaissance and population is rising for the first time in a century.

THE LAST GREAT WHEEL AT ELRIG: MRS. STANHOPE, 1895

This outstanding picture, preserved by Sir Herbert Maxwell in the archives at Monreith House, shows what was, even by 1895, a rare glimpse of an older way of life. The "Muckle Wheel" had actually been in use throughout Europe from the 13th Century. Mrs. Stanhope appears to have been a reluctant subject for the camera, although she is wearing a newly starched apron for the occasion. It appears that her husband had work on the Monreith estate and took visitors to the House out on the White Loch of Myrton to fish.

BEADLE'S HOUSE AND GEORGE INN, MOCHRUM

Here the entrance to Mochrum Kirk shows the Beadle's House, demolished in 1908, and the George Inn, run by J S Thomson; today it is a private house. Mochrum was one of the most architecturally distinguished of South Machars churches, built in 1794 and still containing its original pulpit and sounding board. Sir Herbert Maxwell in *Evening Memories* describes his boyhood visits on a Sunday, when he listened to long sermons, seated in the "laird's loft", although his own family were by this time members of the Irvingite church.

MOCHRUM SCHOOLCHILDREN
The children in this shot of Mochrum are almost all barefoot, although the date is c.1930. The school house still exists, but the school was closed in 1969.

RAVENSTONE CASTLE
A complex structure with many dates, from tower house up to nineteenth century extensions, Ravenstone Castle has connections with the Earl of Galloway's family. After many years of dereliction, it is now being restored.